Greyfriars Bobby

The most famous dog in Scotland

Richard Brassey

A Dolphin ★ Paperback

First published in Great Britain in 2000
by Orion Children's Books
a division of the Orion Publishing Group Ltd
Orion House, 5 Upper St Martin's Lane, London WC2H 9EA

Text and illustrations copyright © Richard Brassey 2000

The right of Richard Brassey to be identified as the author of this work has been asserted.

A catalogue record for this book is available from the British Library

Printed in Italy

ISBN 1 85881 754 4

Greyfriars Bobby is the most famous dog who ever lived in Scotland.

He was so famous that a statue was put up to him in Edinburgh.

He was born about a hundred and fifty years ago, but nobody knows where.
Some people say the Highlands.
Some say Skye.
Some say he was born in the Pentland Hills where his master
was a shepherd.
This is nonsense.

We know that Bobby belonged to an Edinburgh policeman named John Gray. He was a Skye Terrier and his job was to bite the ankles of escaping criminals. Bobby was good at that.

But one bitterly cold winter John Gray fell ill with a terrible fever.
Bobby snuggled close to him to try and keep him warm.

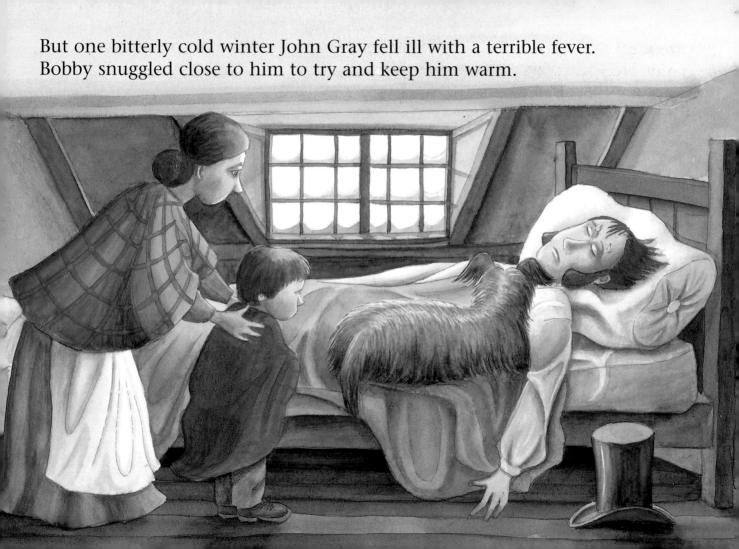

He stayed beside his master even when John Gray died.

He followed the funeral procession to Greyfriars churchyard.

Bobby stayed on after the last mourner went home.
He watched as the grave was filled in. He stood on the
bare earth and howled. When night came he
crept under a gravestone to keep guard.

The days came and went, and still Bobby refused to leave his master's grave.

Dogs were not really allowed in the churchyard, but James Brown, the gardener, felt sorry for Bobby and let him stay. On cold nights he even invited him in. But Bobby would never desert his master for long.

When spring came, Bobby chased away all the cats in the churchyard. Mr Brown was pleased.

The cats had been a nuisance.

Bobby soon made plenty of other friends. There were the poor
people, whose crowded houses backed on to the churchyard . . .
the boys of Heriot's School, who climbed over the wall . . .

the owners of all the nearby eating houses . . . and a soldier who used to take him up to the castle to see the gun, which was fired off every day at one o'clock.

Bobby soon got into the habit of setting off for dinner at the sound of the one o'clock gun. People gathered each day to see him trotting past. The story of the faithful dog had spread all over Edinburgh.

One day a new owner arrived at Bobby's favourite restaurant. Mr Traill was not from Edinburgh and had never heard of Bobby, but he realised that many people paid to eat there just to see him.

HIS MASTER WAS A SHEPHERD. HE DIED IN MY ARMS.

I'VE KNOWN HIM SINCE HE WAS A PUPPY.

He gave Bobby lots of extra tasty food, to make sure he came every day. He even made up stories about Bobby for anyone who asked.

The most important person in Edinburgh was the Lord Provost. When he heard the story, he was touched by Bobby's faithfulness.

He announced that he would pay Bobby's licence for life. He gave him a special collar with a brass plate.

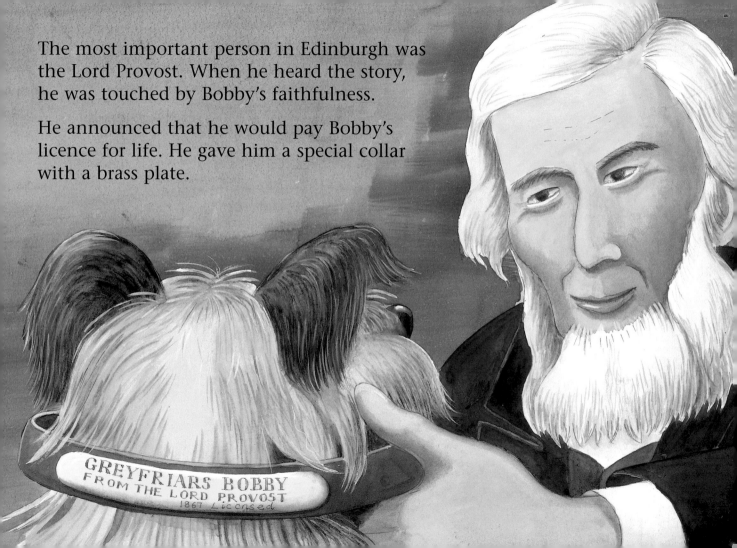

GREYFRIARS BOBBY
FROM THE LORD PROVOST
1867 Licensed

The story was reported in all the newspapers. Greyfriars was soon crowded with sightseers, painters and photographers.

A lot of nonsense has been talked about Bobby over the years.

Some people said he never existed just because they couldn't find him when they visited the churchyard.

Others, who wouldn't have known a Skye Terrier from a poodle, pronounced that Bobby was a Scotty.

Some people just wanted to make a name for themselves.

A journalist made headlines by claiming he had invented the whole story after a vicious dog chased him from the churchyard . . .

and Mr Traill went on making up stories about Bobby until his dying day.

It's not surprising that when an American lady decided to write a book about Bobby she got many things wrong. It didn't help either that she had never been to Scotland and made most of it up. But the book was very popular and years later Walt Disney made a film based on it.

Whatever people may say about Bobby, we know enough to be sure that he did exist.

At Huntly House Museum in Edinburgh you'll find his collar, his bowl and a real photo of him, looking rather old and sad. You'll even find a photo of Mr Traill and his family with Bobby.

Bobby spent fourteen years faithfully guarding his master's grave. When he died, he was buried in a flowerpot in front of Greyfriars church. A hundred years later, a stone was put up to mark the spot.

Even today there are people who say they see him, chasing cats in the churchyard.